Coloring book for adults and kids amazing dress image for design

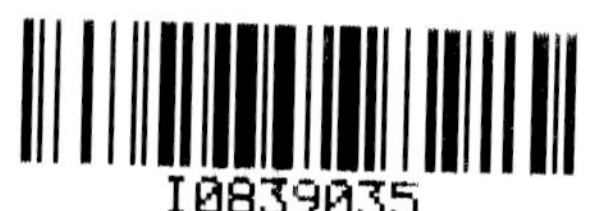

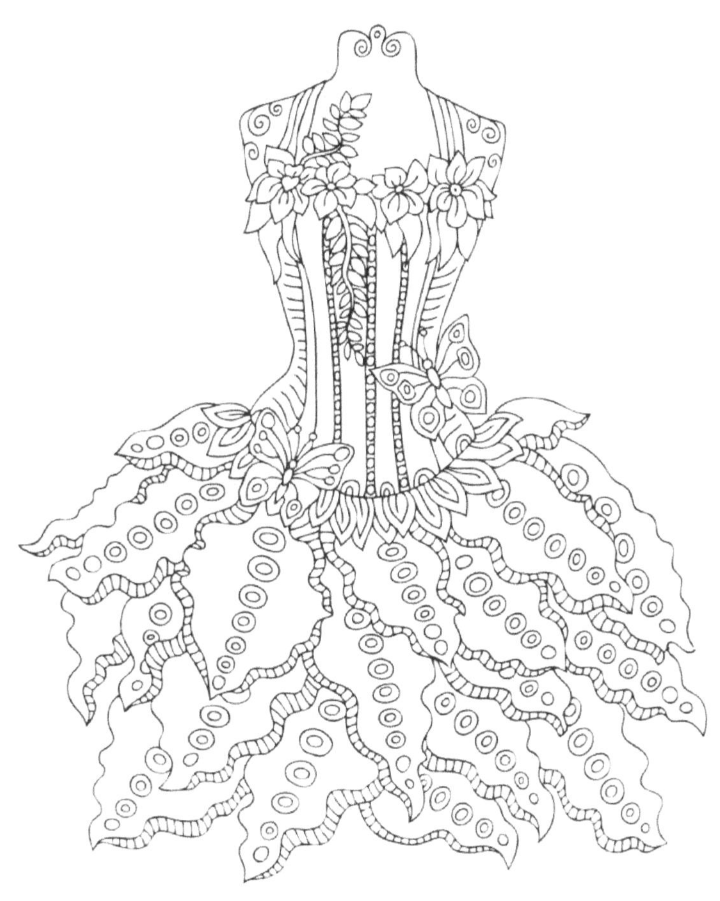

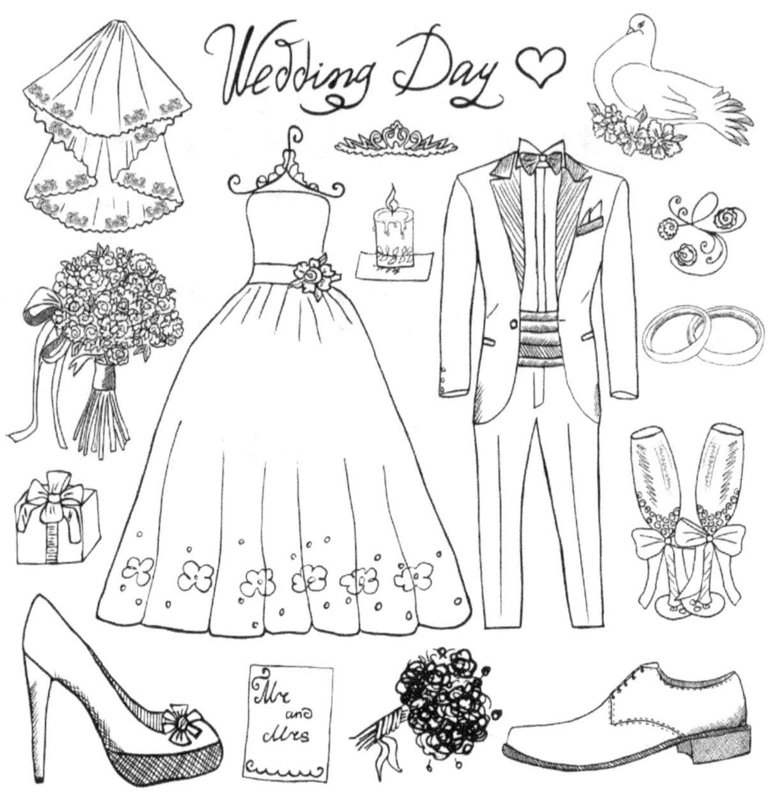

This coloring book is belongs to

____

____

____

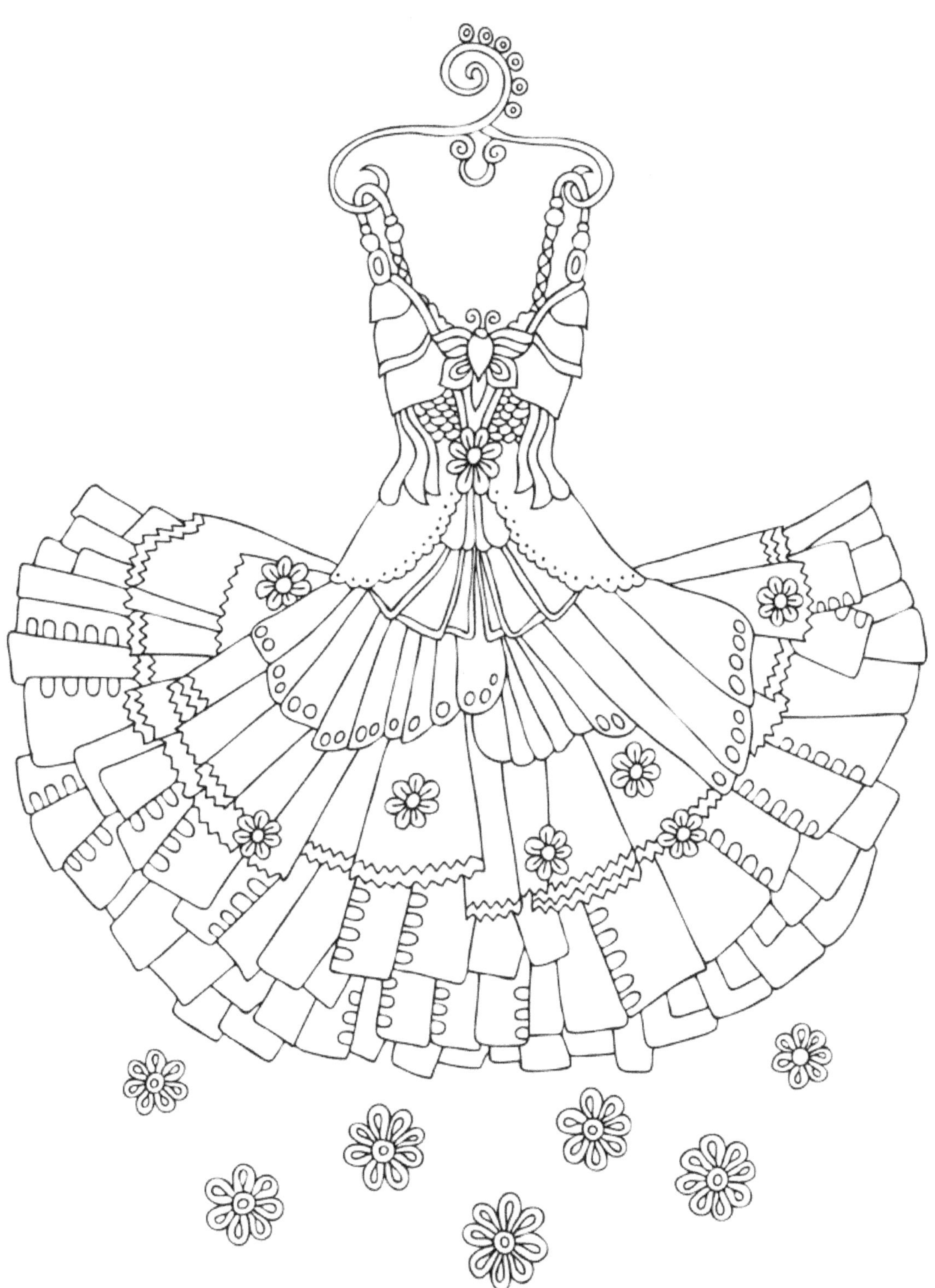

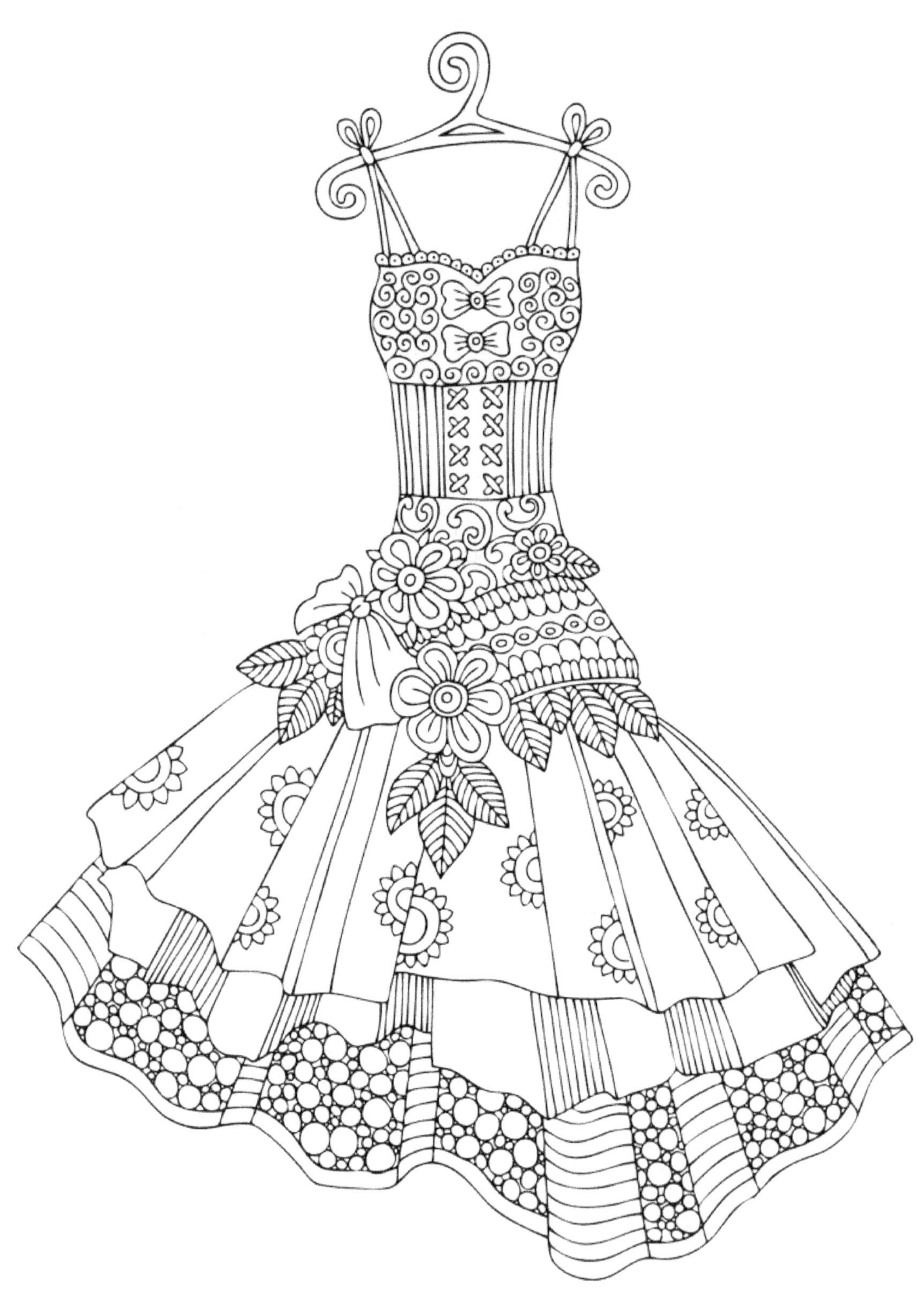

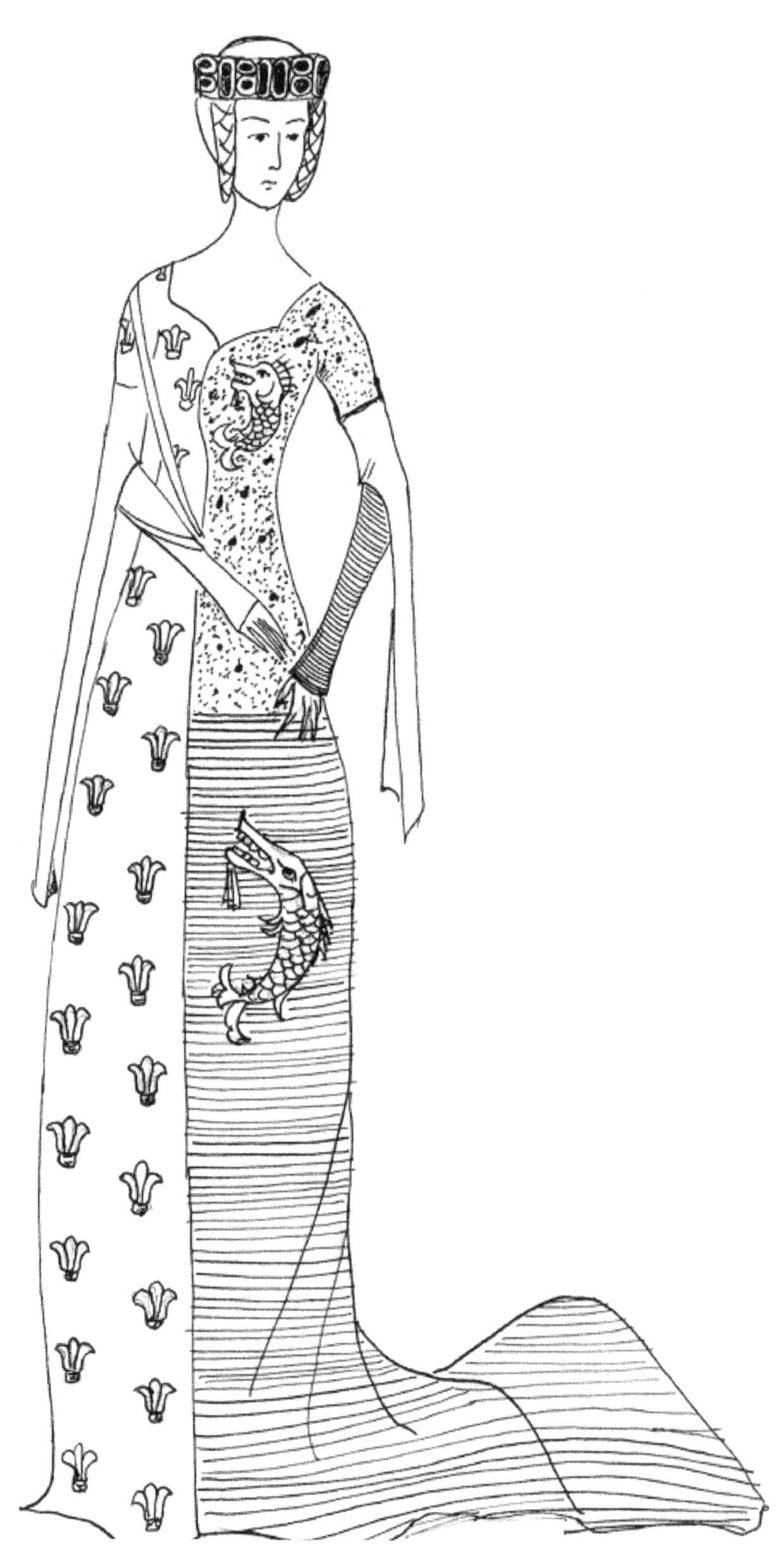

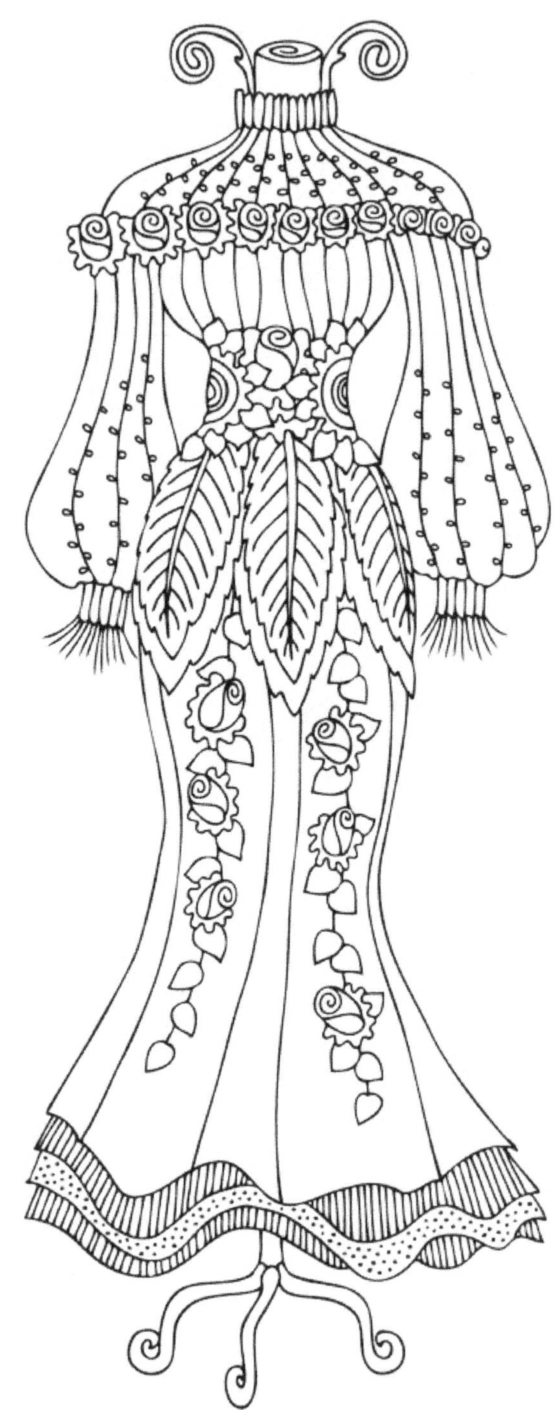

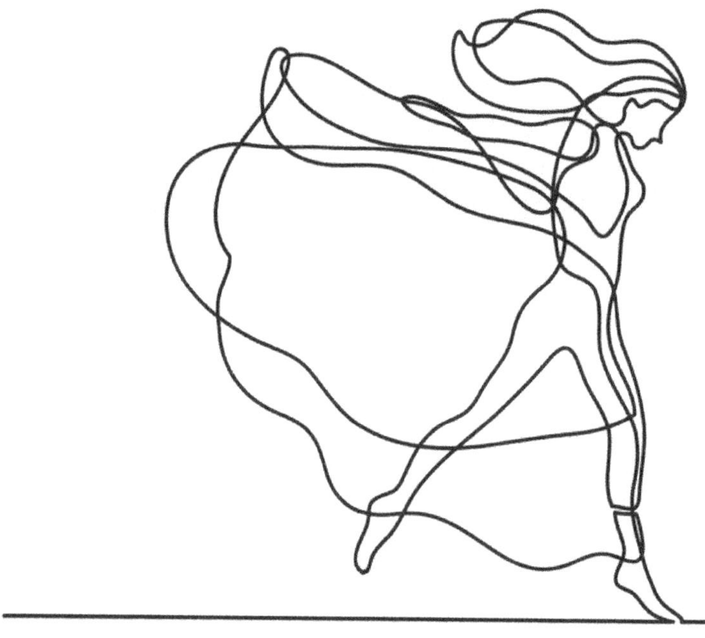

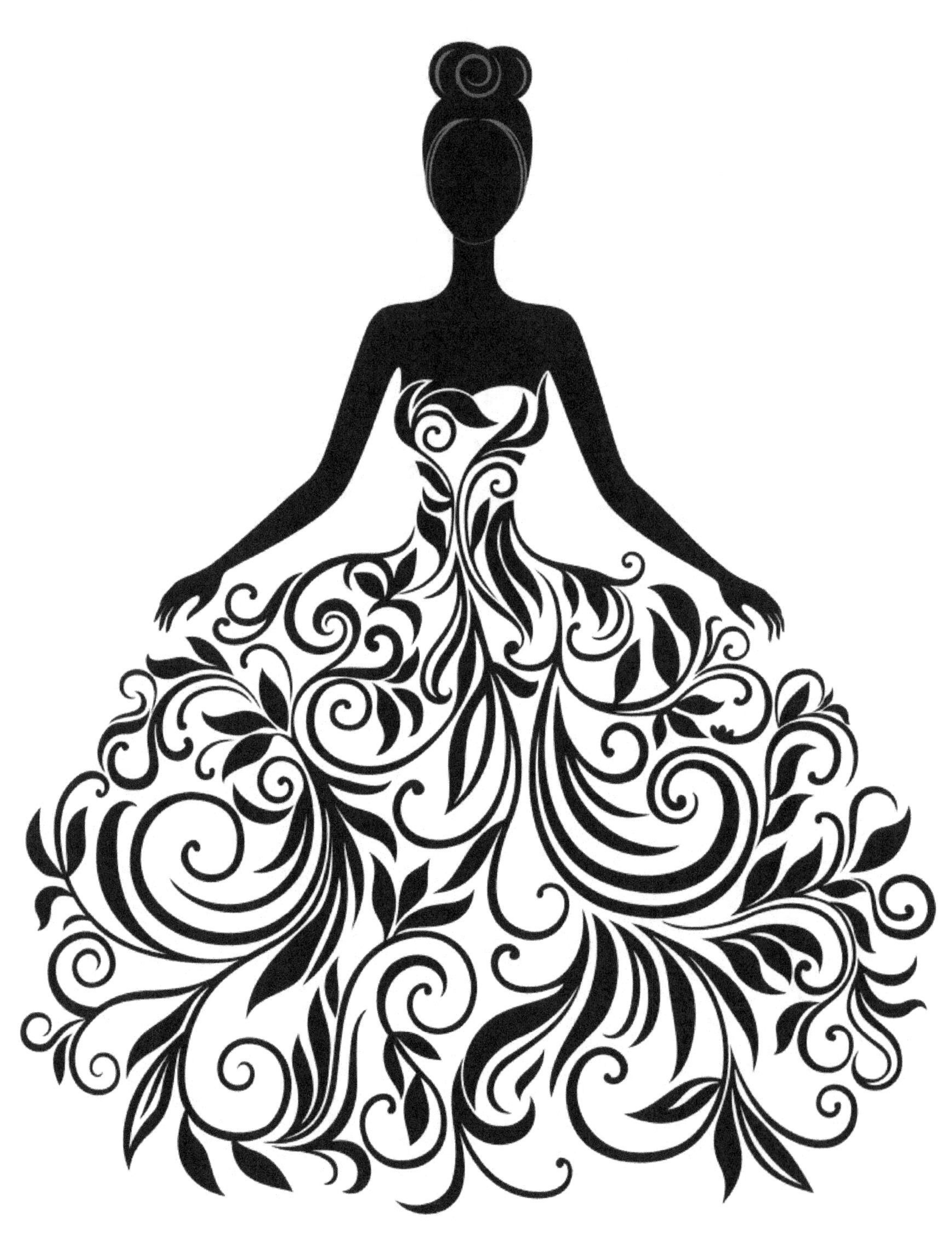

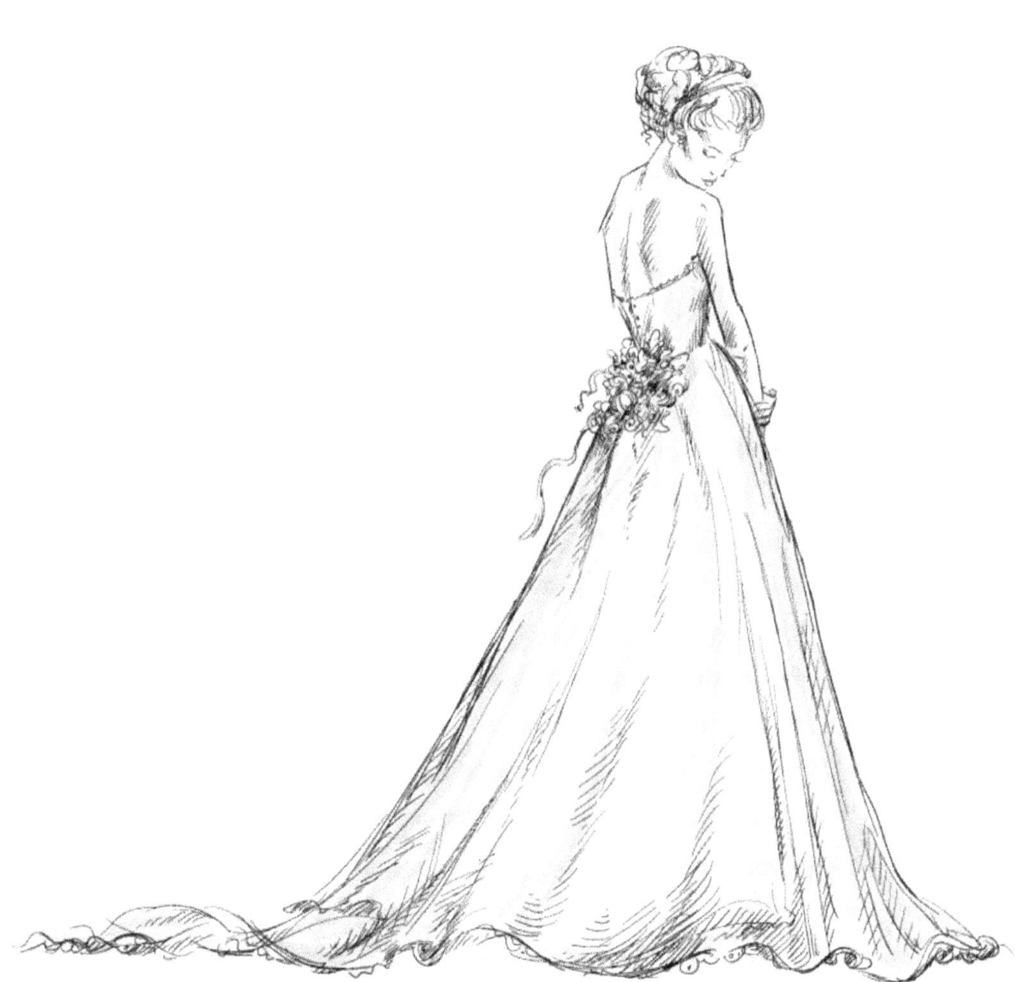

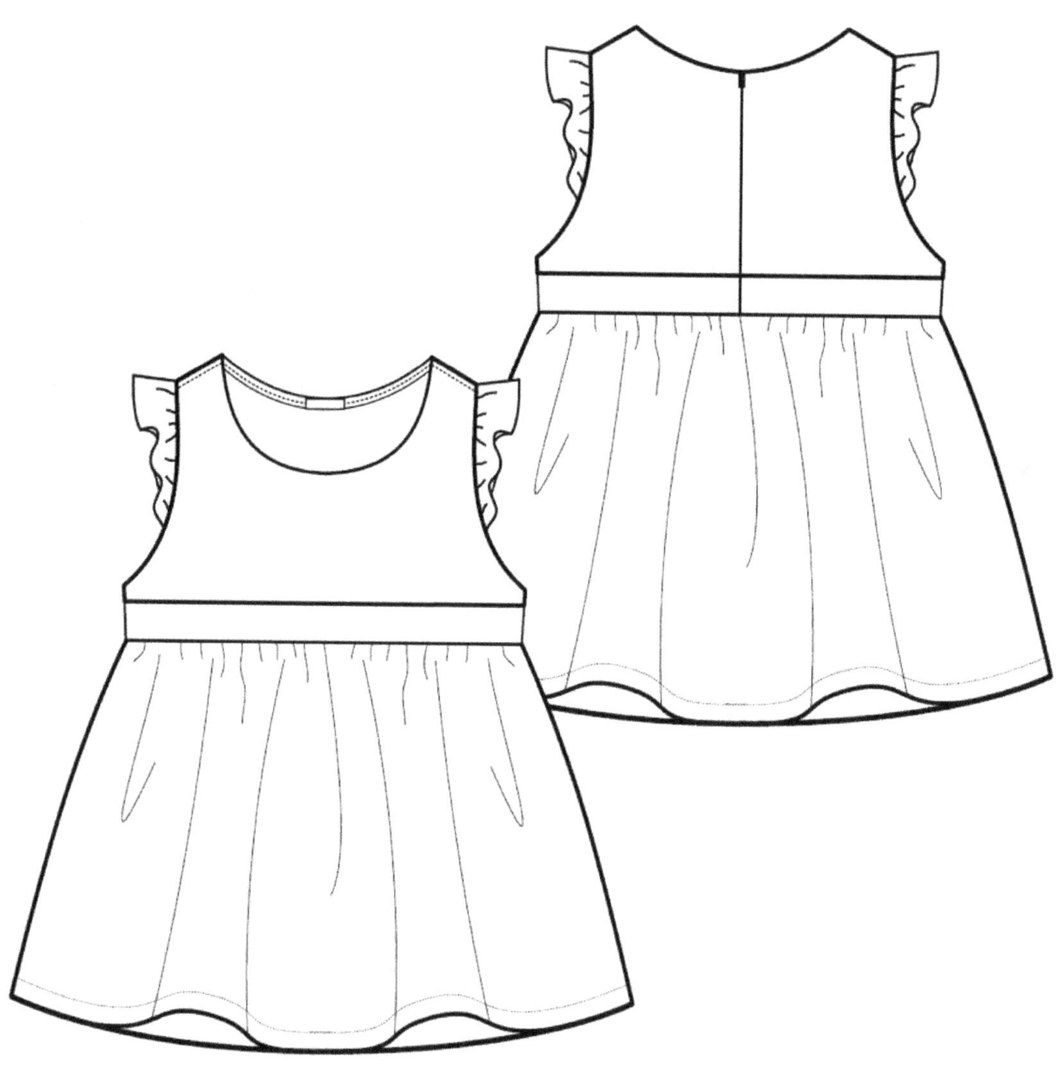

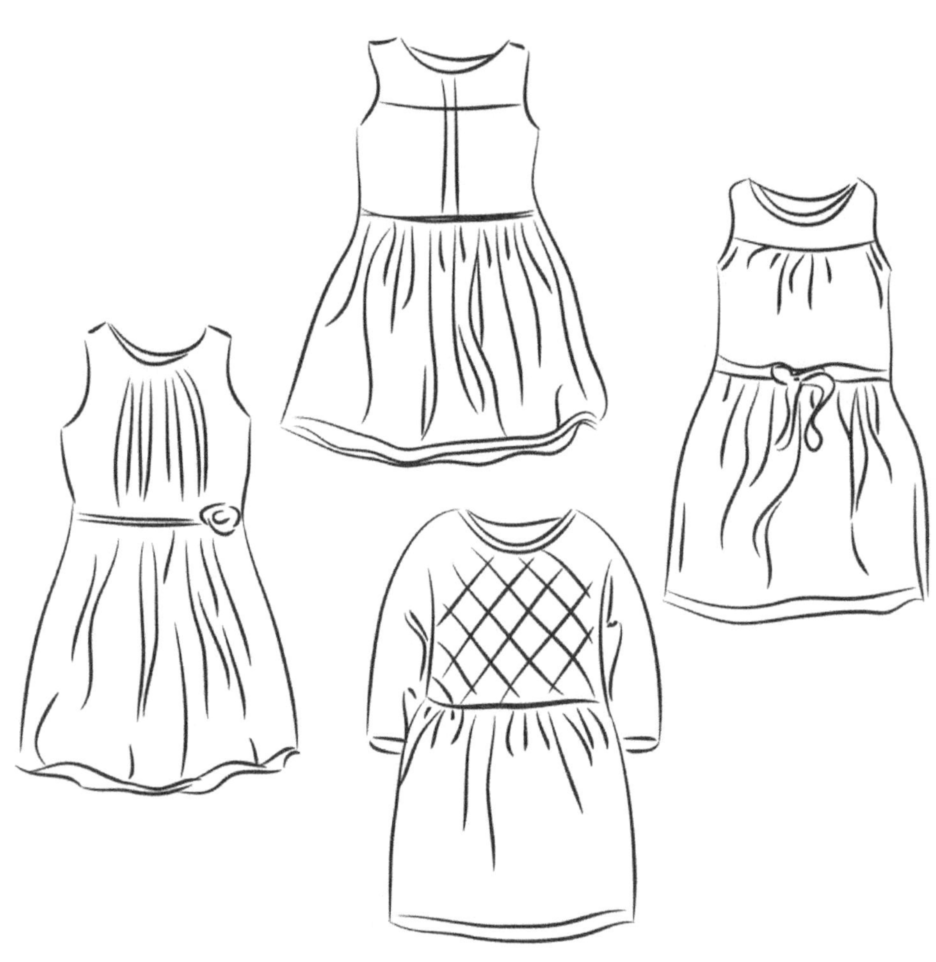

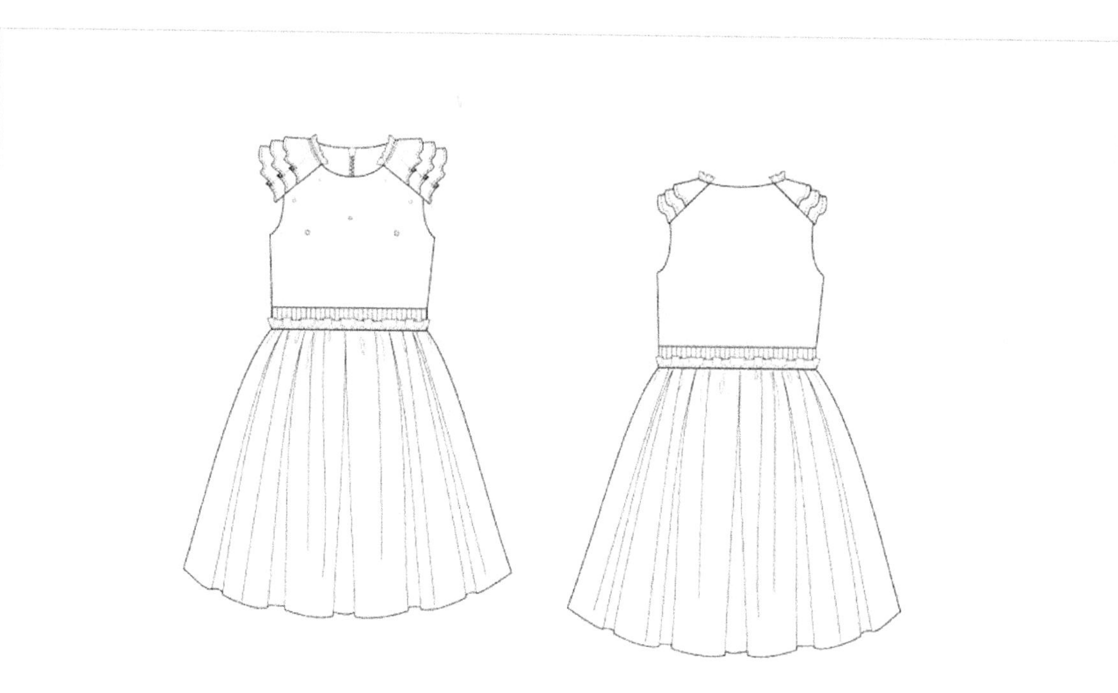

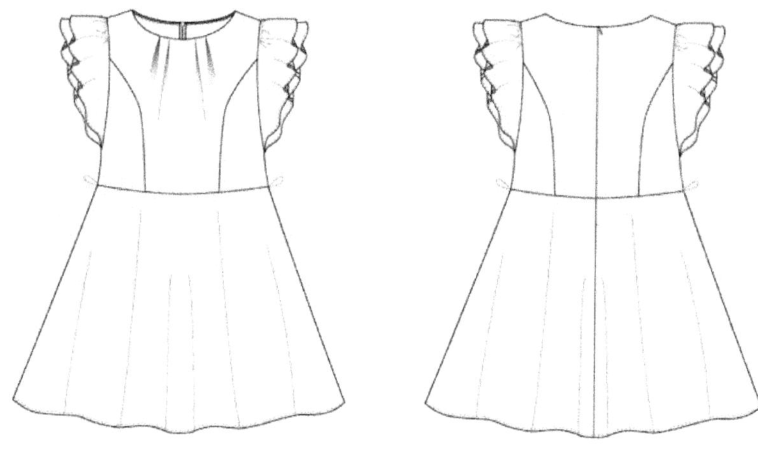

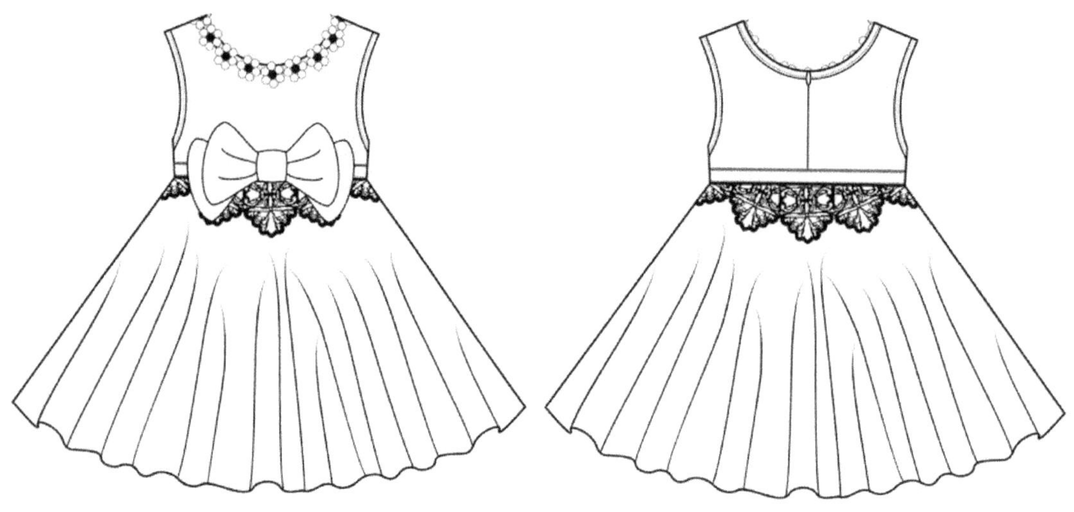

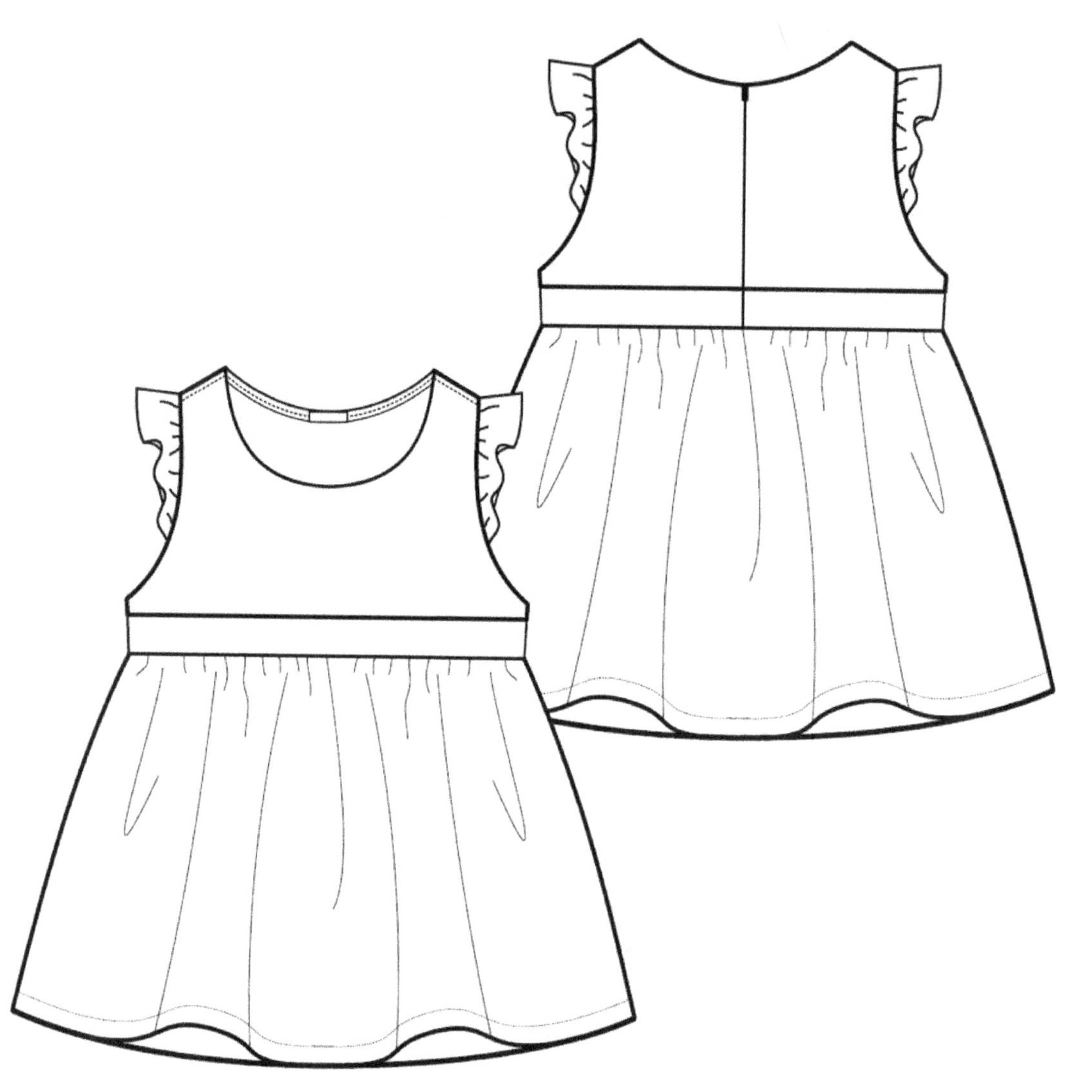

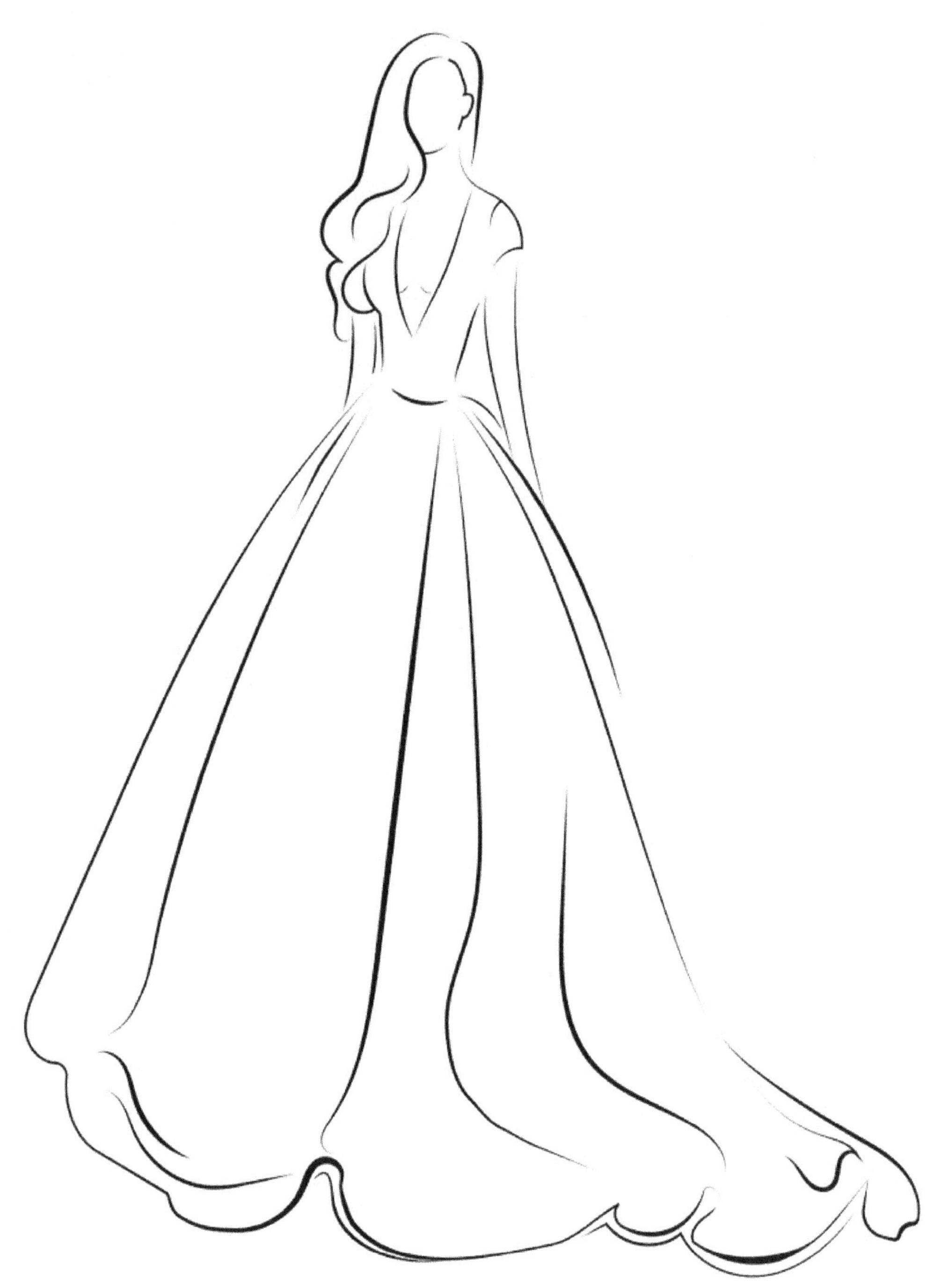

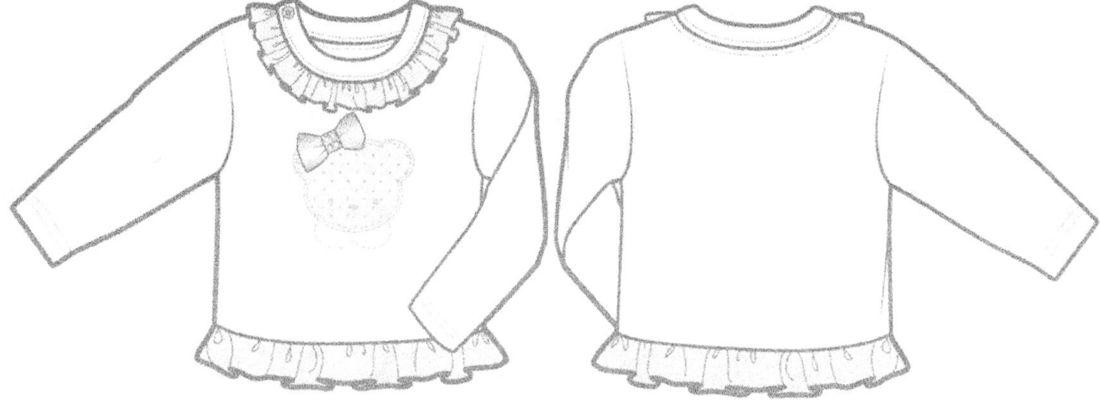

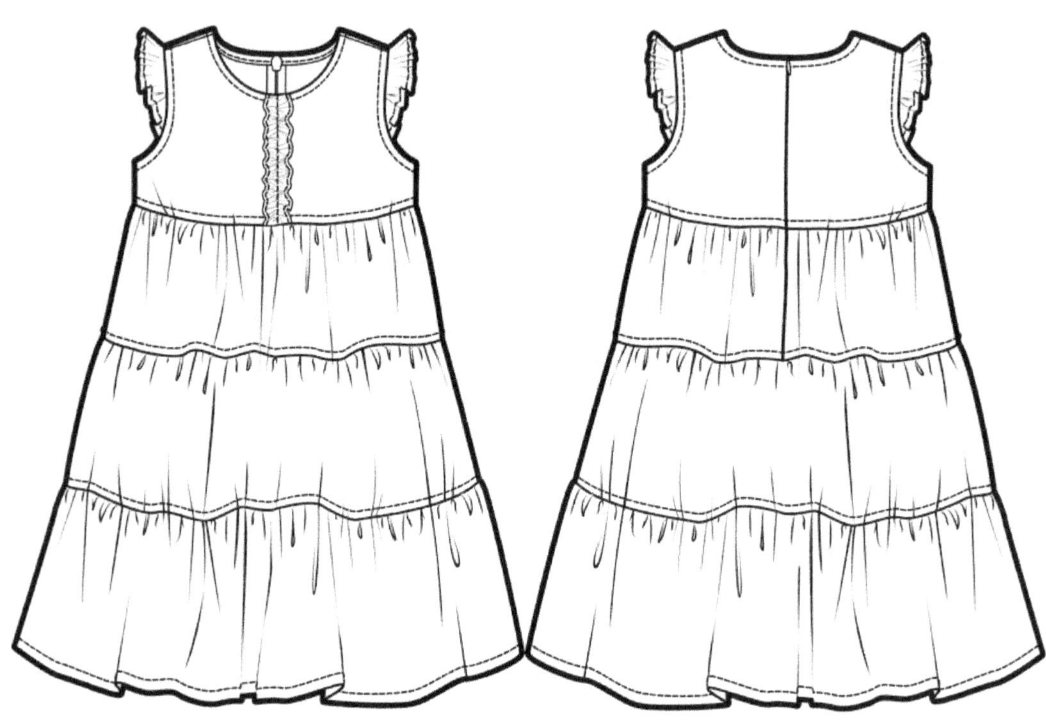

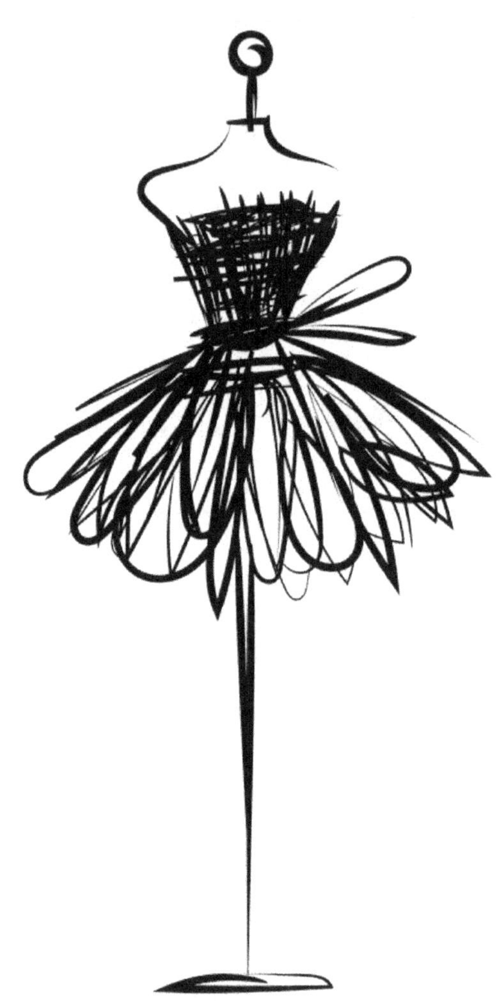

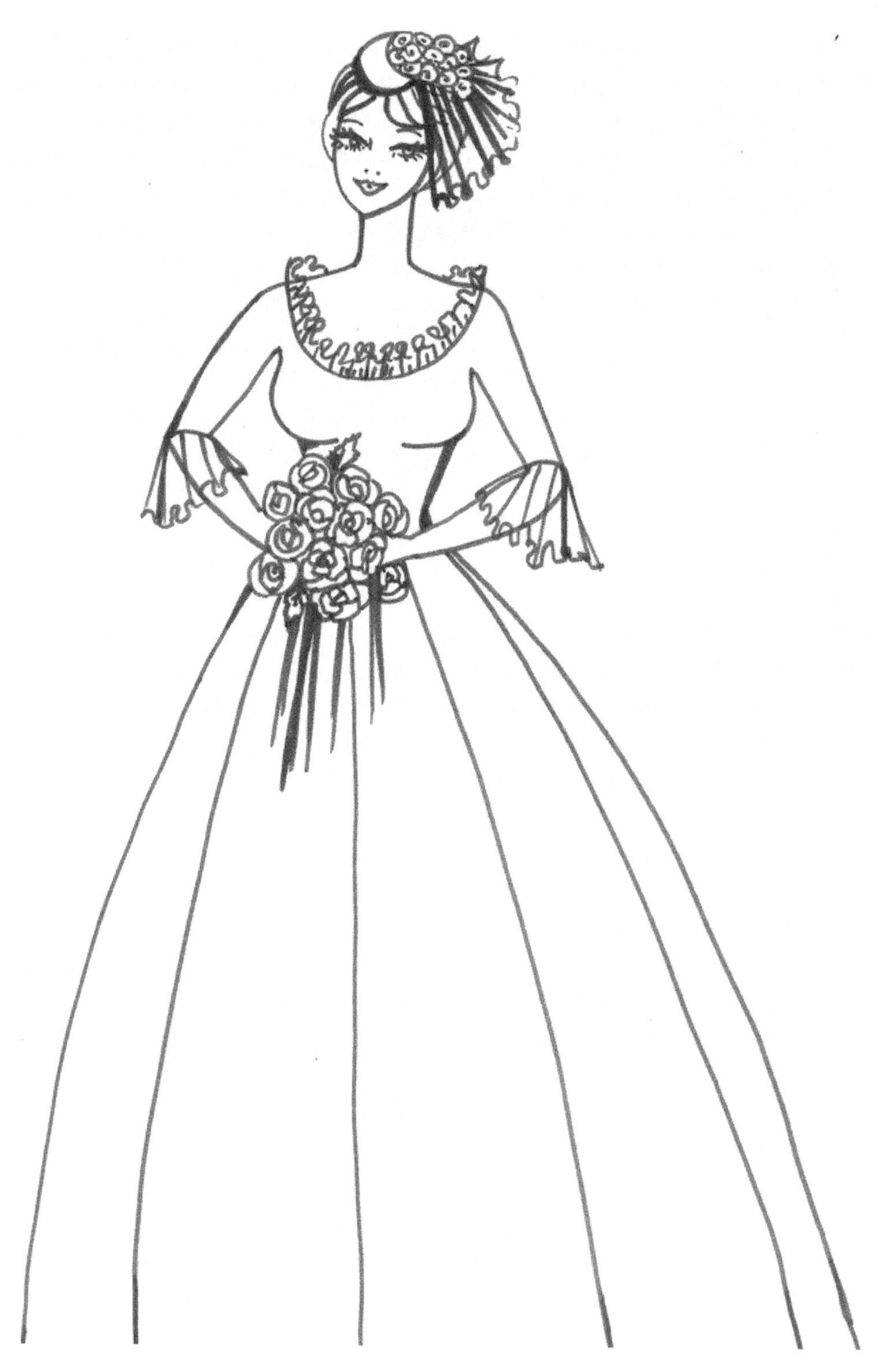

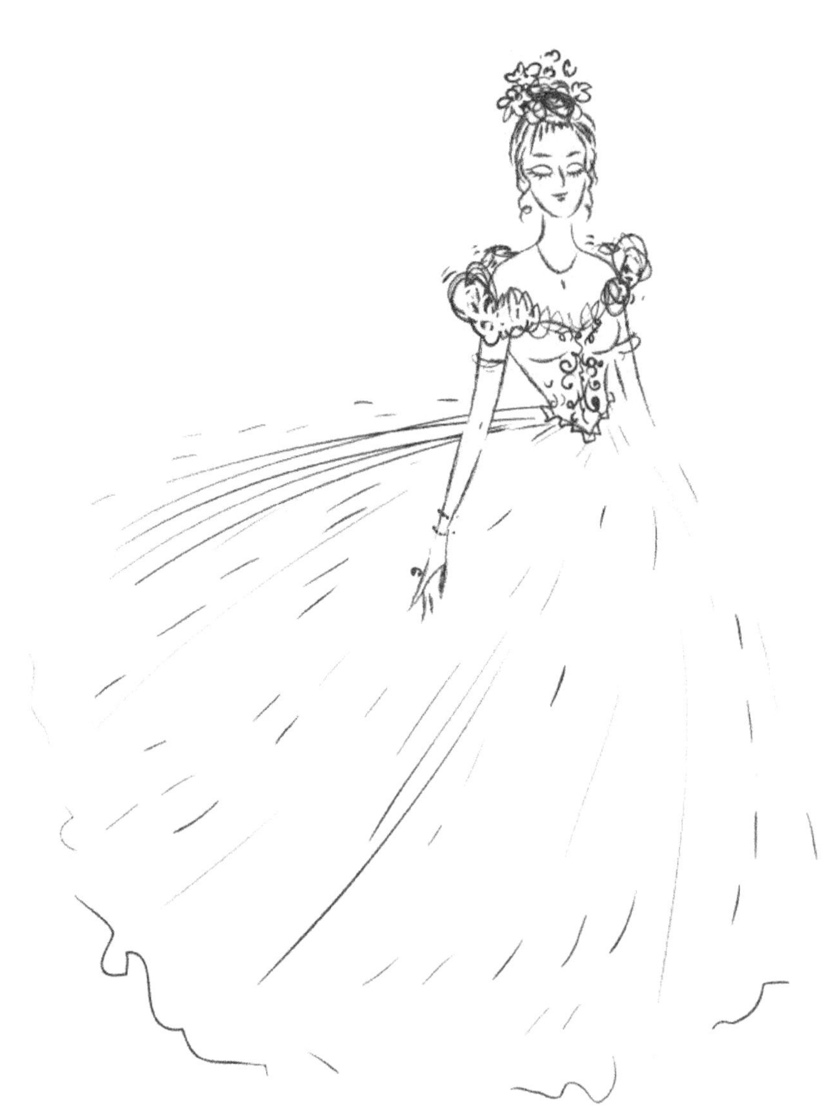

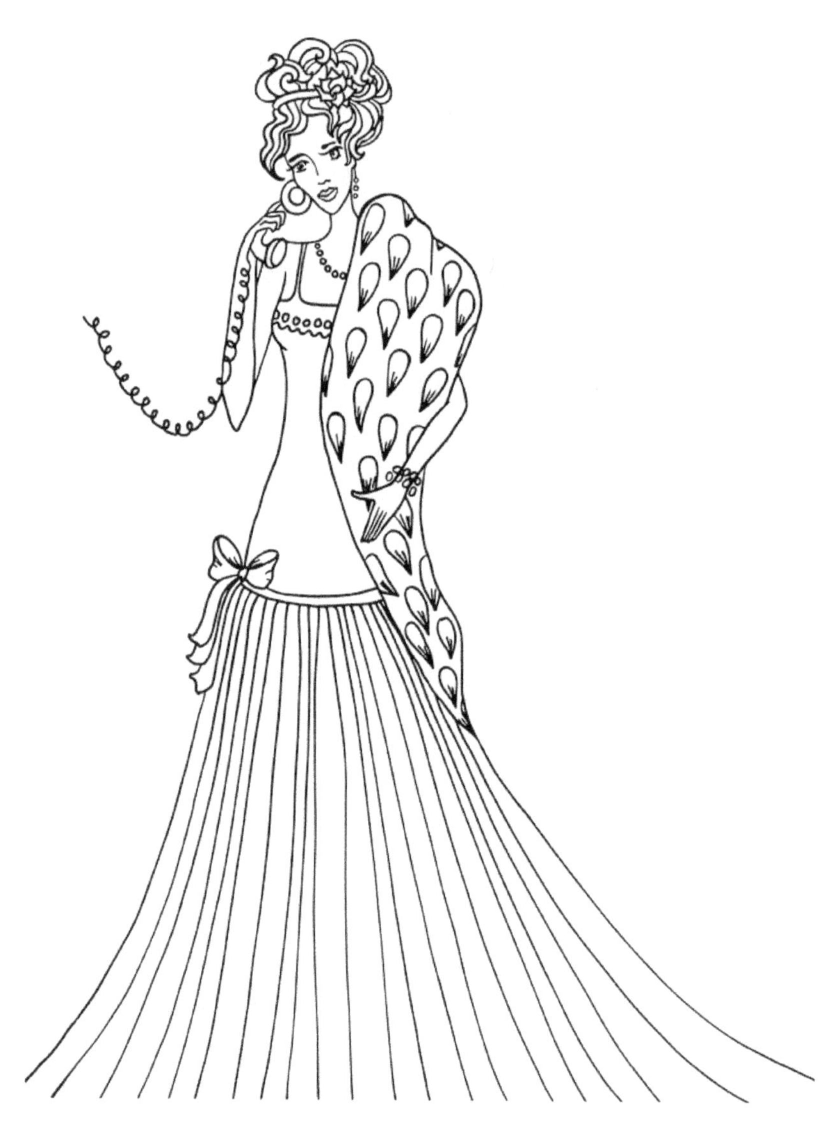

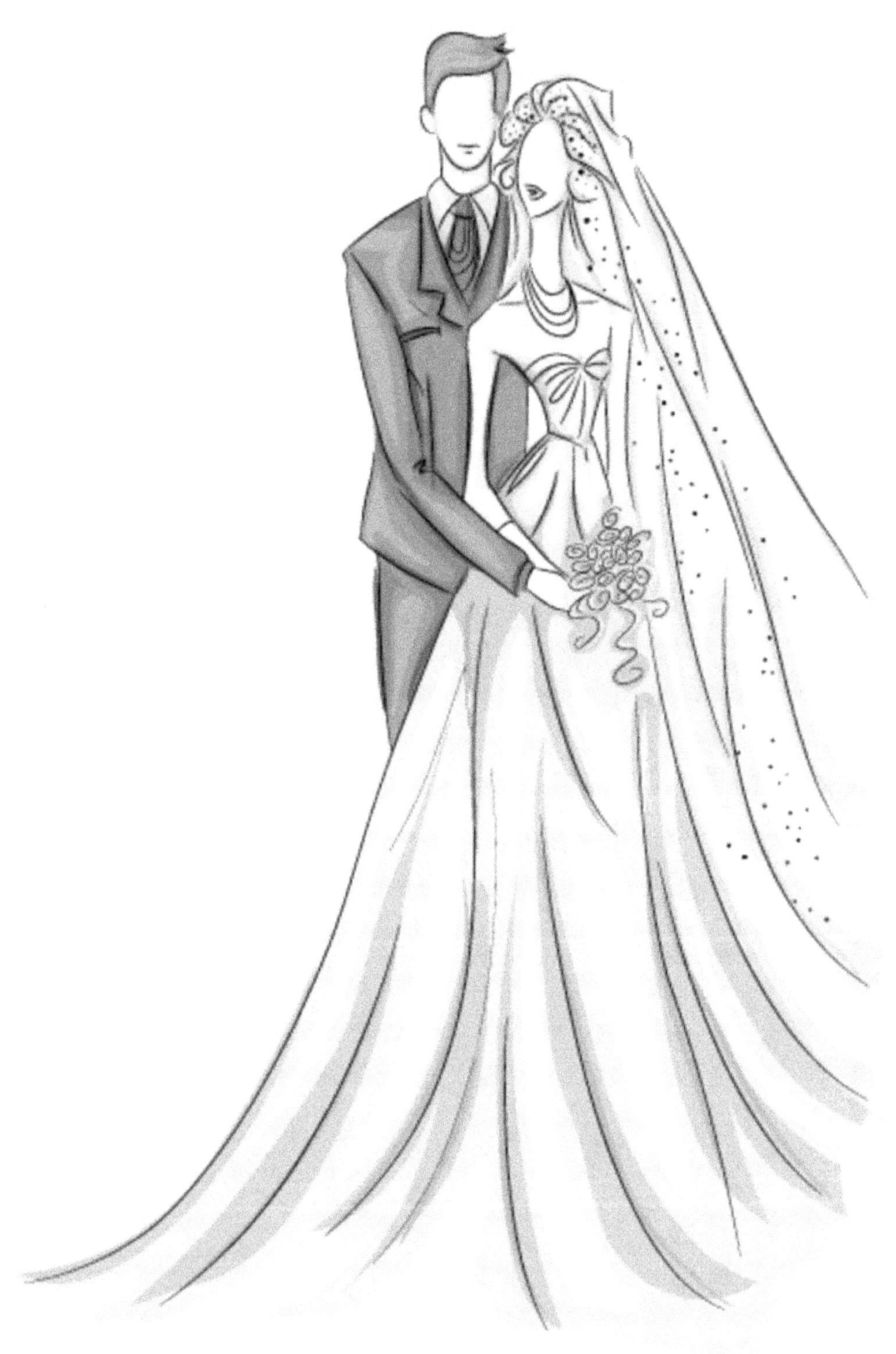

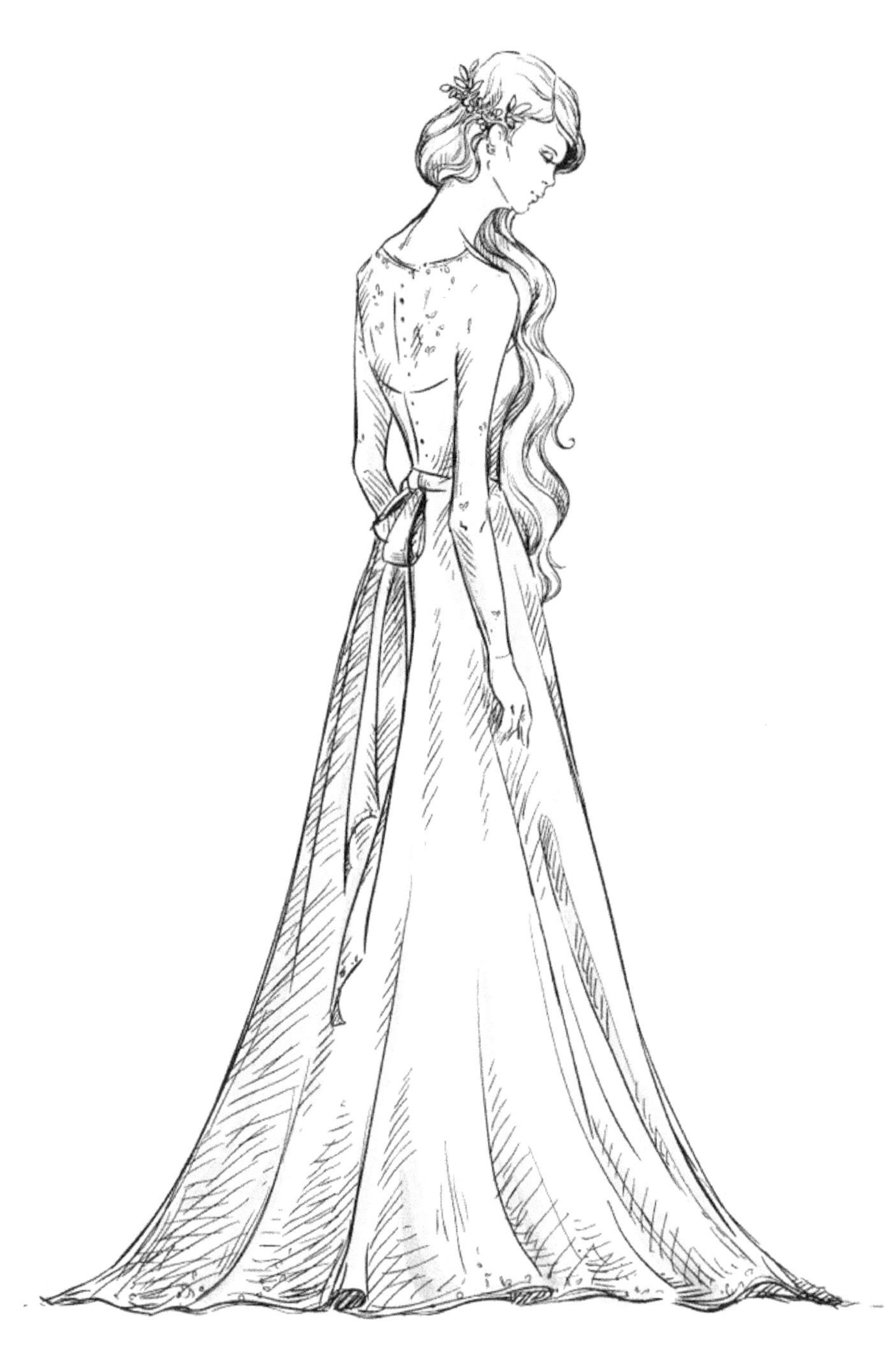

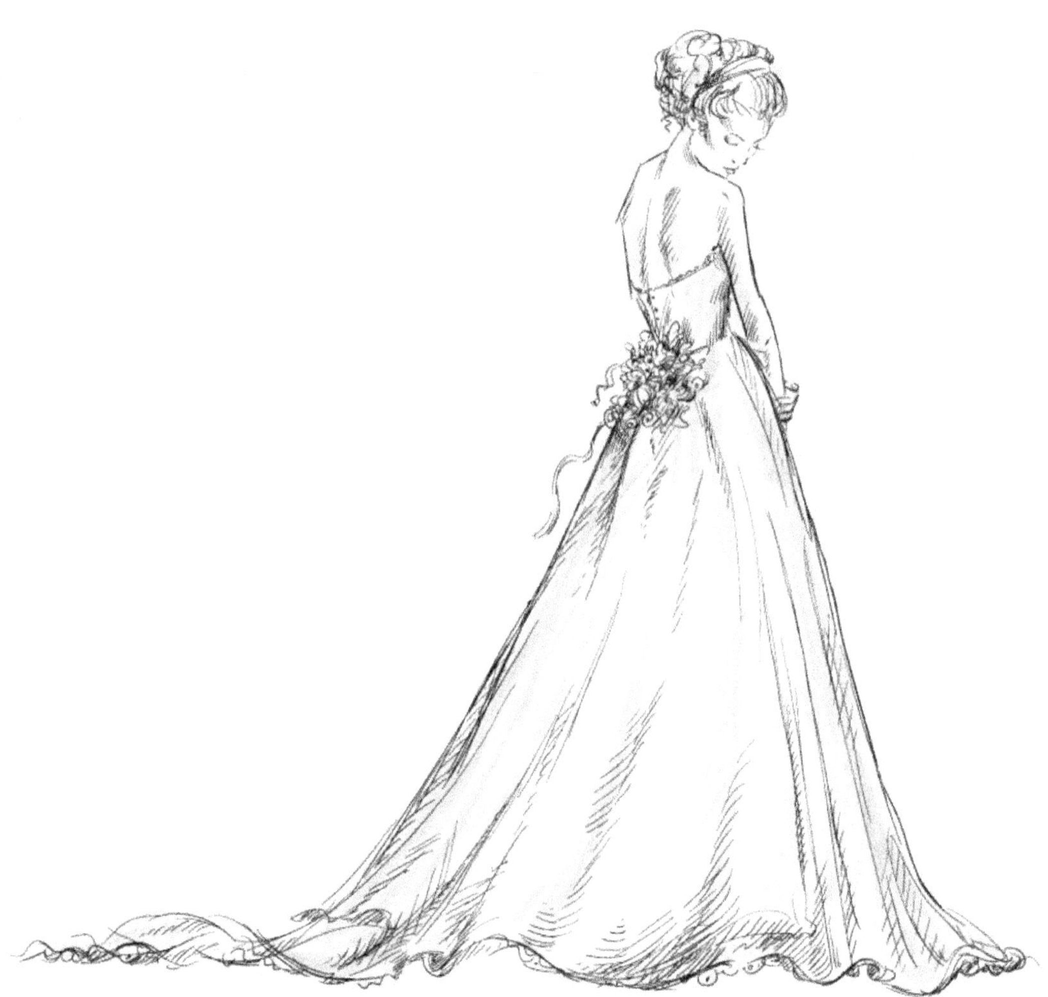

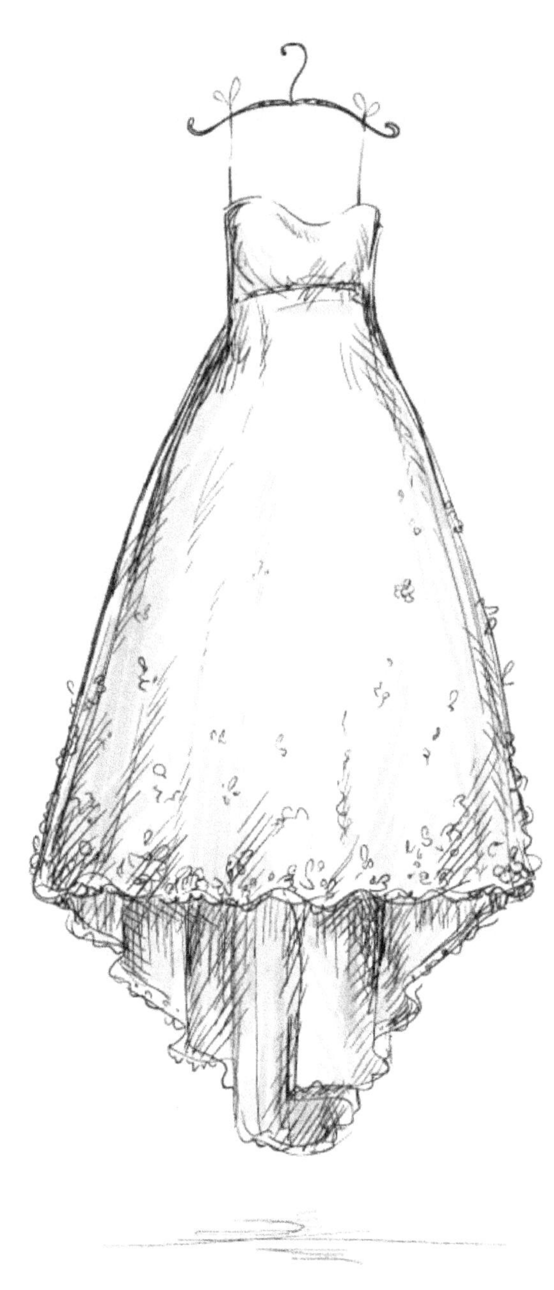

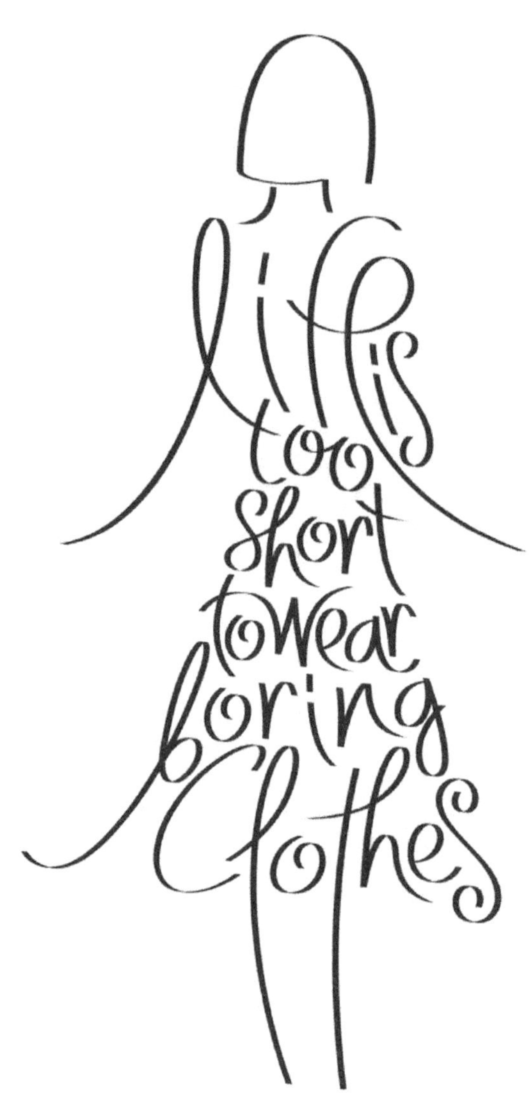

life is
too
short
to wear
boring
clothes

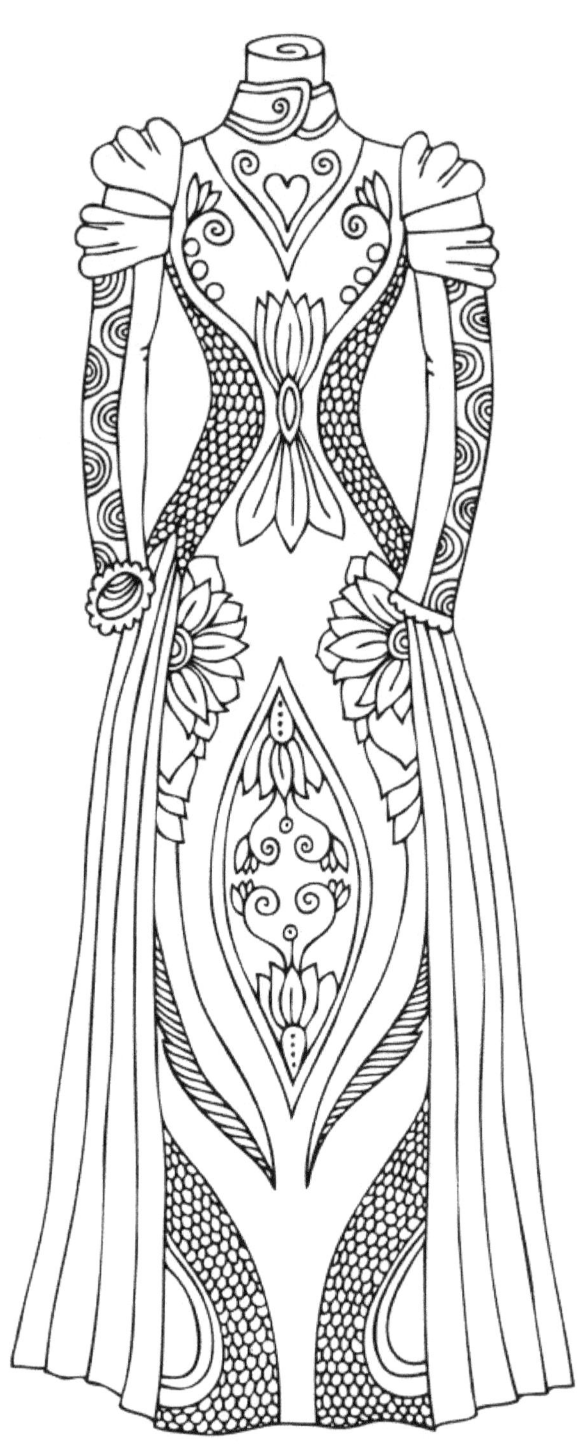

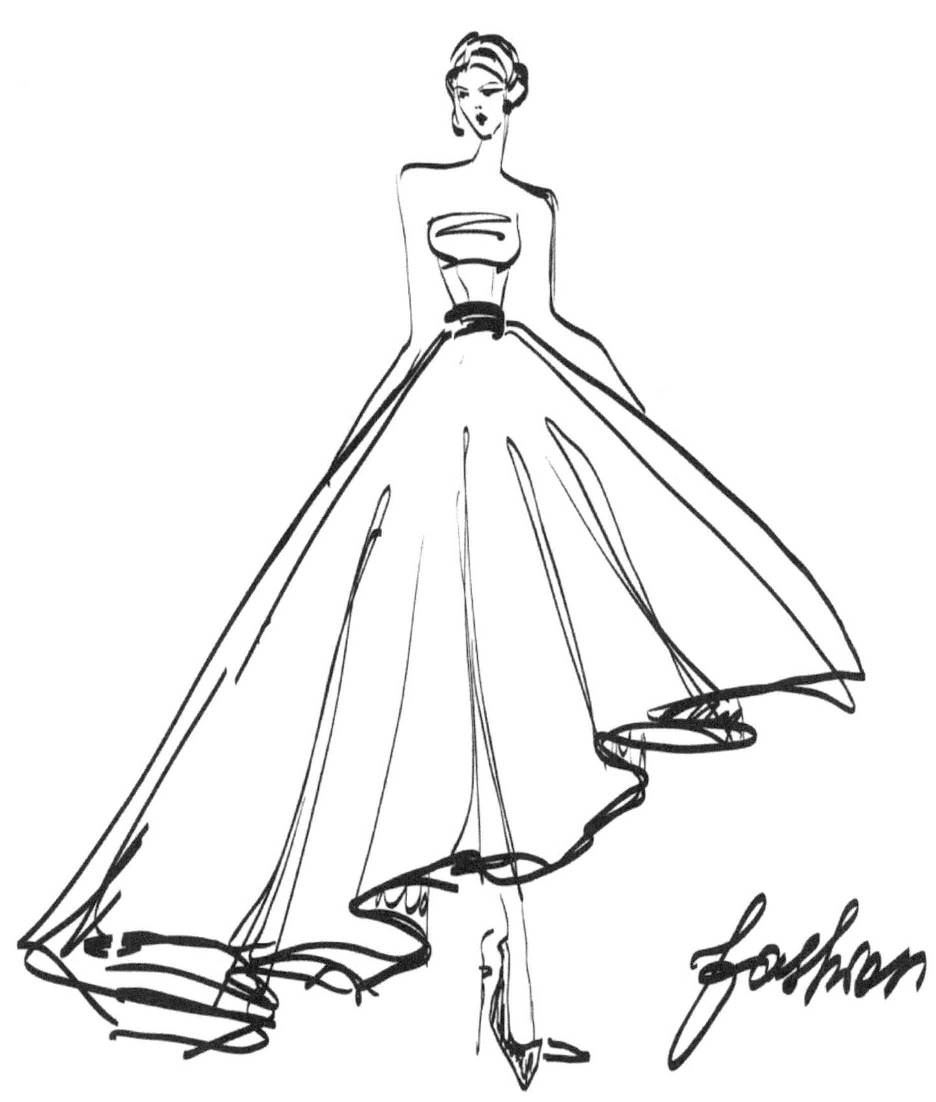

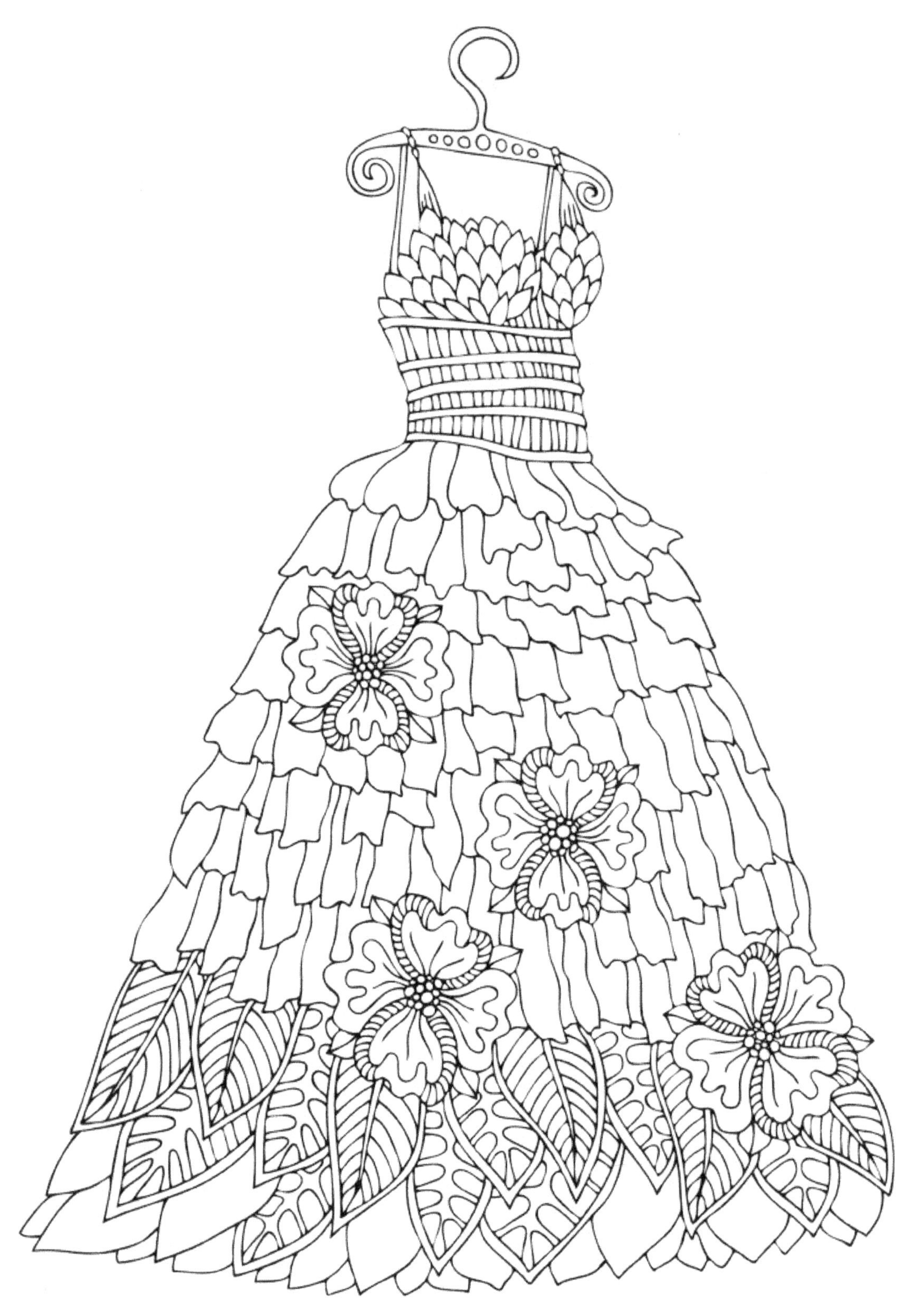

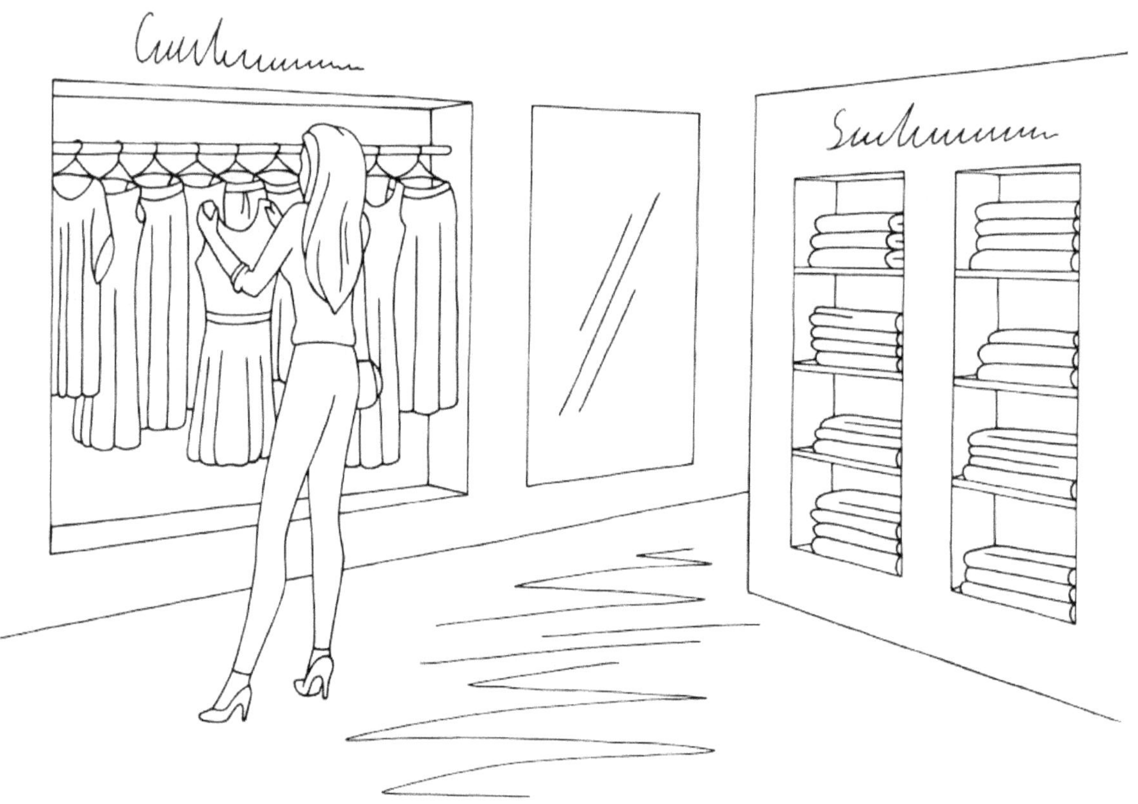

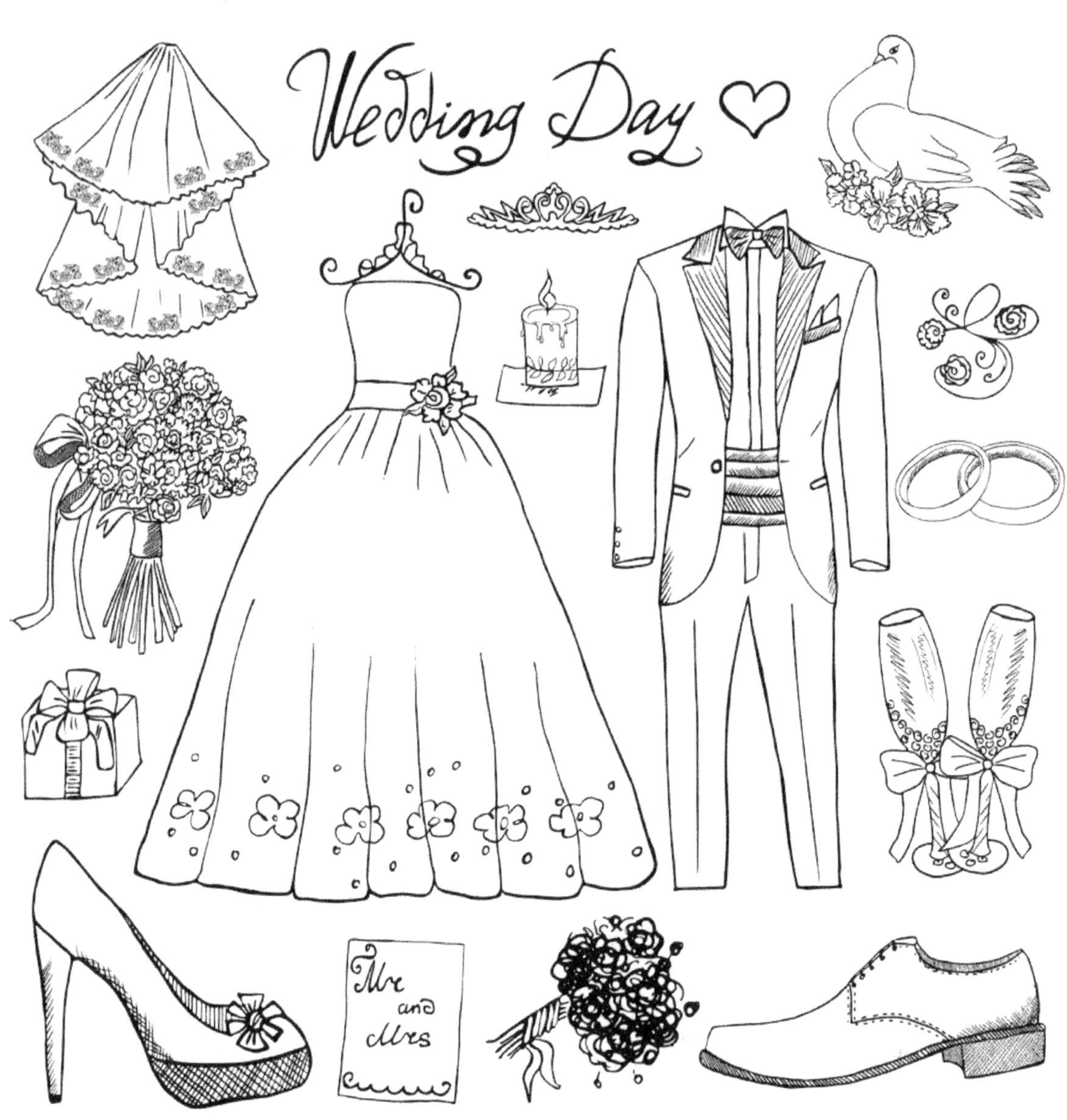
Wedding Day
Mr
and
Mrs

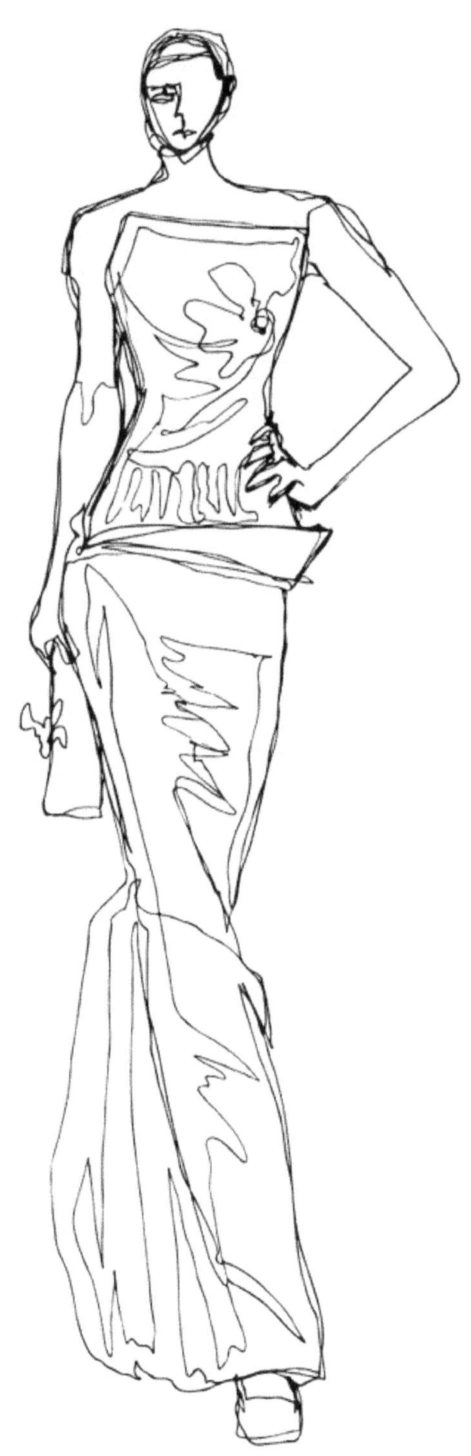

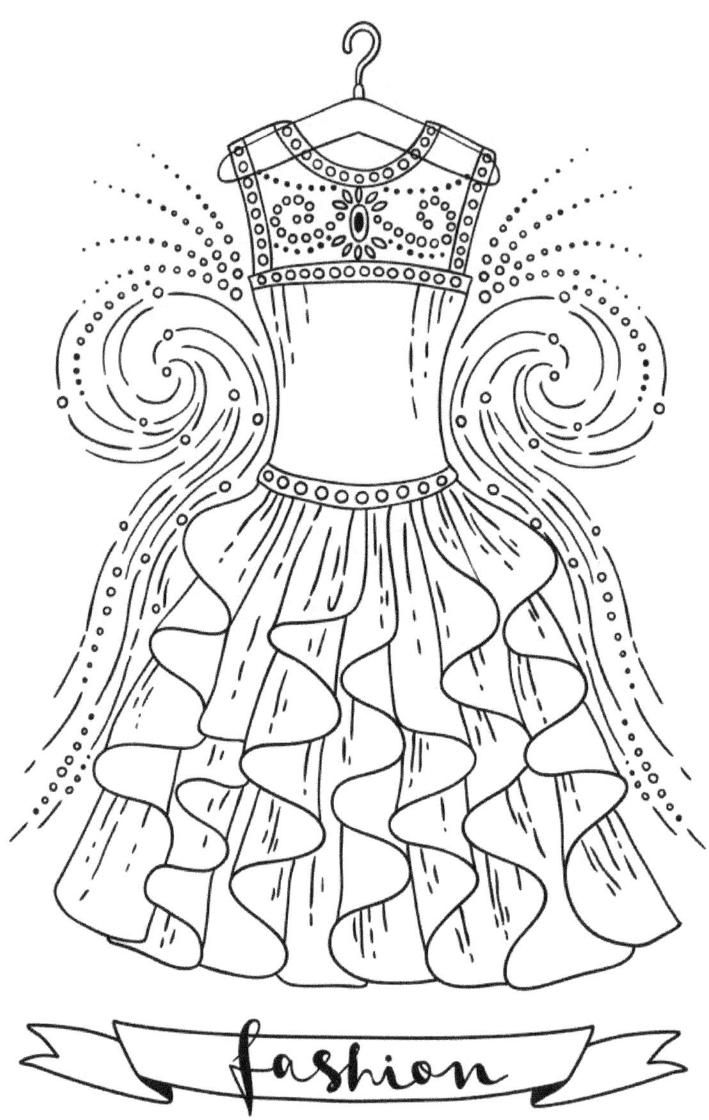

fashion

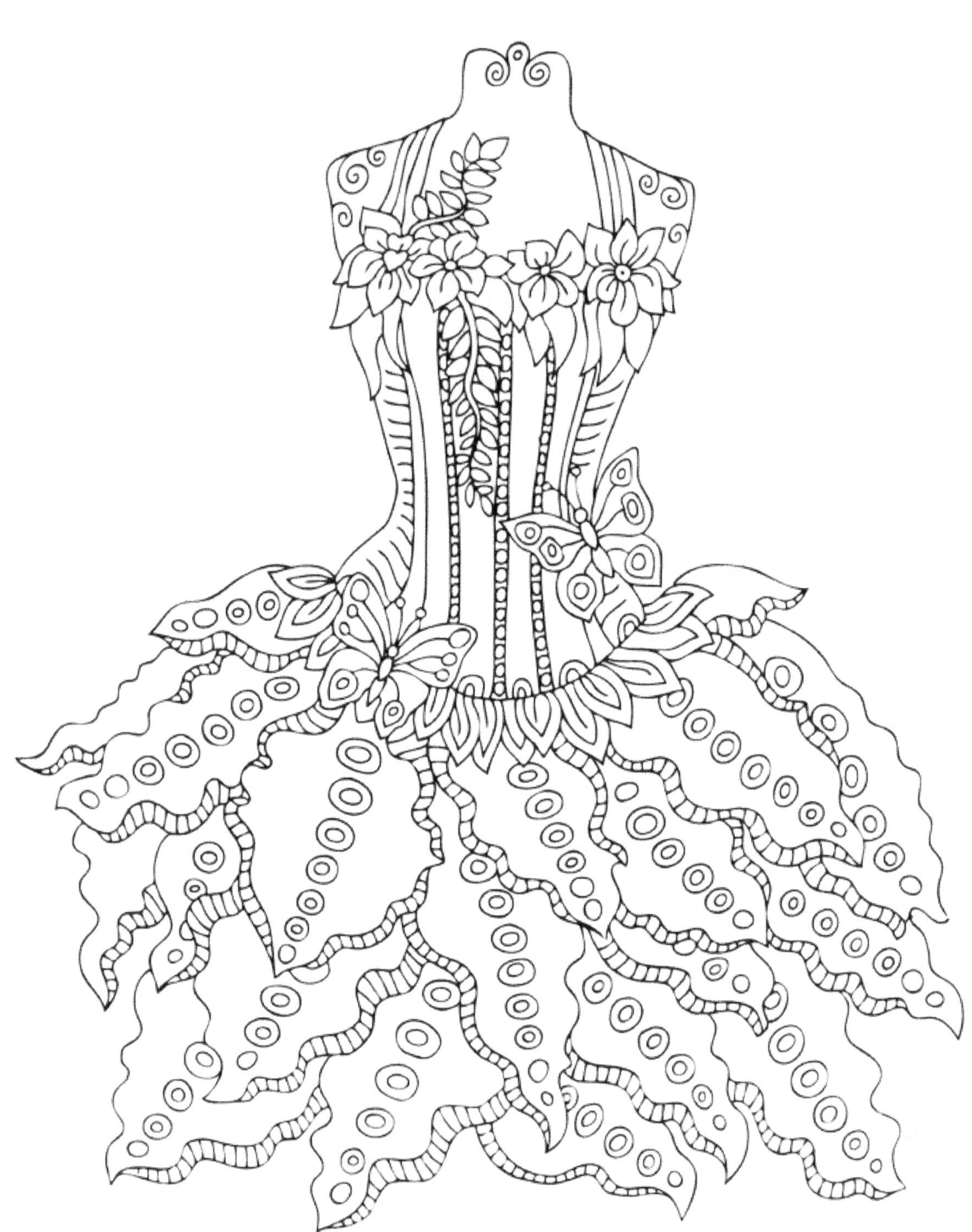

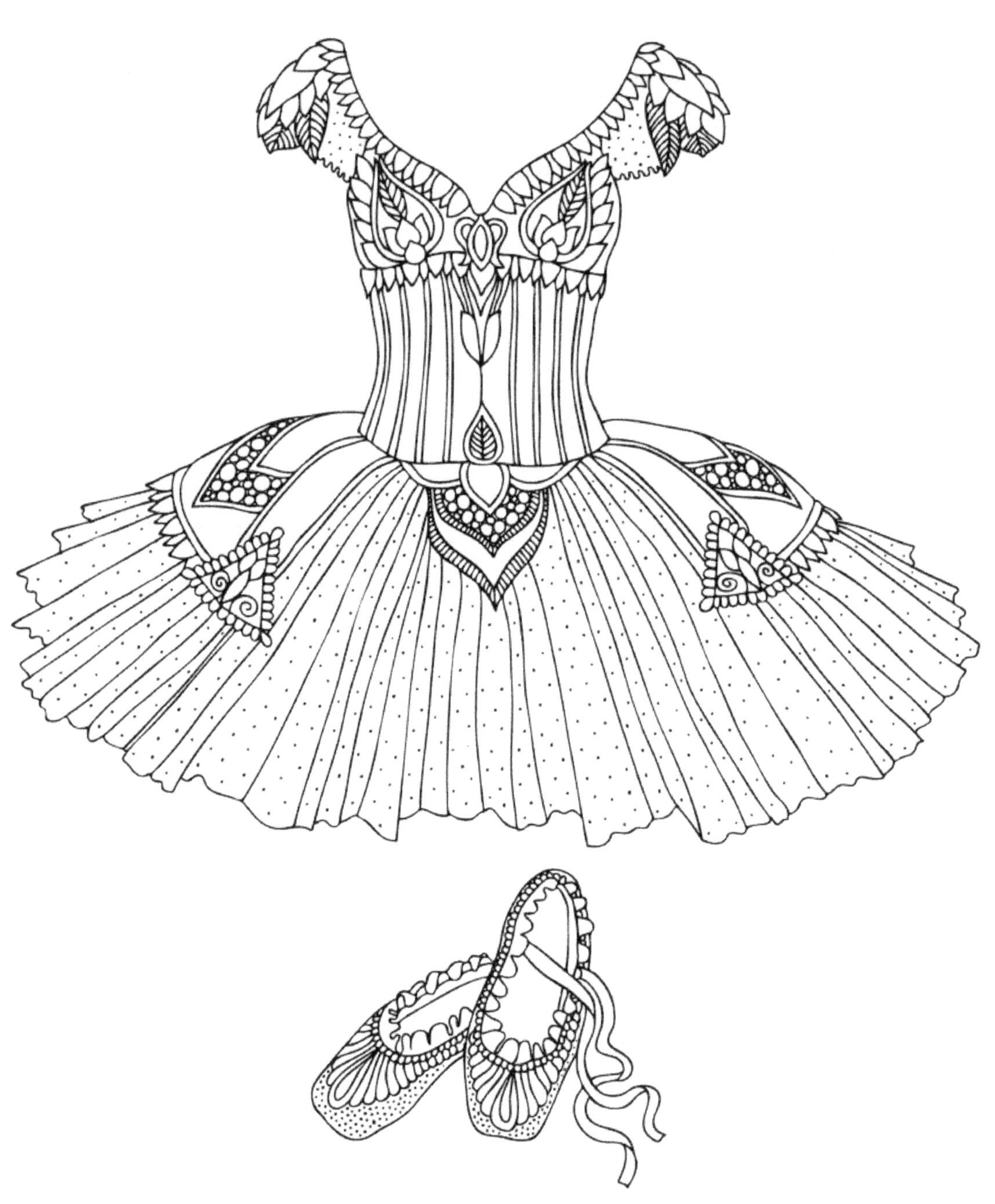